■SCHOLASTIC

Teaching With Favorite
Lois Ehlert
Books

BY PAMELA CHANKO

NEW YORK • TORONTO • LONDON • AUCKLAND • SYDNEY
MEXICO CITY • NEW DELHI • HONG KONG • BUENOS AIRES

Teaching *Resources*

For Samantha and Gillian,

the flowering buds

on my family tree.

ACKNOWLEDGMENTS

Many thanks to Kama Einhorn, a great editor and a great friend.

Jacket illustrations from *Red Leaf, Yellow Leaf, Eating the Alphabet,* and *Planting a Rainbow* used by permission of Harcourt, Inc. All rights reserved.

Front cover and interior design by Kathy Massaro
Interior art by James Graham Hale

ISBN: 0-439-59719-6
Copyright © 2005 by Pamela Chanko.
All rights reserved.
Printed in the U.S.A.

4 5 6 7 8 9 10   40   13 12 11

Contents

About This Book

Through simple text and dazzling artwork, author-illustrator Lois Ehlert creates books that make the world of nature come alive for children—and make its processes and cycles accessible to even the youngest learner. Whether introducing basic concepts (such as ABC's in *Eating the Alphabet* or numbers in *Fish Eyes*) or more complex ideas (the life cycle of a butterfly in *Waiting for Wings*), Ehlert's love of the natural world shines through all her work. Her layered collage illustrations draw children into the artist's world, allowing them to see through her eyes the beauty in a leaf, a flower…and even a green vegetable! The intricate, tactile nature of her artwork also appeals to the way young children learn—through touch and through exploration. Each time you open a Lois Ehlert book, children are bound to notice something new. In addition to the main story lines, many of Ehlert's books include identifying labels for plants and animals as well as glossaries with more detailed information on the final pages. This makes the books perfect to share with readers at varying levels, which is exactly the author's aim.

Having grown up with a younger brother and sister and shared the same books, Ehlert knows that each reader looks at a book in a different way, and takes away different things from the experience. She also notes, "I always liked books with lots of things in them, so I could read them more than one time and notice different things." It is evident from the author-illustrator's work that she still notices "different things"— not only in books but also in the glorious details of the world around her. Her books provide a venue for children to notice these details as well, allowing them to discover new and exciting aspects of their environment on every page.

The activities in this book are designed to help you get the most out of Lois Ehlert's work by extending children's literature experiences to many curricular areas, including math, science, language, dramatic play, art, and social studies. On page 6 you will find activities to use with any Lois Ehlert book; on the pages following, you will find activities to use with 13 specific titles. For each featured book, you will find:

◎ **About the Book:** Summary and book description.

◎ **Concepts and Themes:** Important ideas addressed in the story.

◎ **Before Reading:** Ways to tap children's prior knowledge and prepare them for the literature experience.

◎ **After Reading:** Discussion tips for enhancing children's learning, deepening their understanding, and helping them relate the story to their own lives.

◎ **Extension Activities:** Cross-curricular activities to help you reinforce and expand on children's learning.

On the last page of this book, you will also find culminating activities for a Lois Ehlert celebration. Whether you choose to do a full author study or dip into her stories from time to time throughout the year, this book is sure to help you bring Lois Ehlert's already vibrant work even further to life in your classroom!

About Lois Ehlert

Lois Ehlert was born on November 9, 1934, in Beaver Dam, Wisconsin. Born into a creative family, she says that she "grew up in a home where everyone seemed to be making something with their hands." Her mother was a good seamstress, and her father had a carpentry workshop in the family's basement. Both parents supported her desire to create, providing her with sewing and carpentry scraps and a work space of her own. She did a lot of drawing and painting, but never liked either quite as much as cutting and pasting her scraps—an affinity that is still evident in her work today. Reading was also an important part of life in the Ehlert family. Ehlert visited the local library every week with her brother and sister, checking out the maximum number of books allowed each time. "There's nothing more exciting than learning to read," the author states. "It's almost magic. It opens all the doors."

After graduating from high school, Ehlert attended the Layton School of Art as a four-year scholarship student. She also did graduate work at the University of Wisconsin-Milwaukee. She went on to work professionally as a graphic artist and also tried her hand at illustrating other authors' books. She found that she didn't like the restrictions, however, and eventually moved on to writing and illustrating her own books. When asked how she comes up with ideas, she has said that she writes and draws things that she knows and cares about: She grew up with a garden, and still presses maple leaves in her phone book each year. She has enjoyed making snow creatures, and a squirrel really did sneak its way into her house one day. Says the author, "With paper and glue, and my trusty scissors, I express the simple things of life—the homely, ordinary subjects that I love."

Ehlert's favorite subjects may come from the world of the everyday, but her work is far from ordinary. She has a knack for expressing the childlike wonder of discovering the world. Her children's books have earned her numerous awards, including a Caldecott Honor for *Color Zoo* and a *Publisher's Weekly* Best Book of the Year for *Snowballs*. She now lives in Milwaukee, Wisconsin, but still maintains close ties to her home community—three large banners designed and made by Ehlert hang in the Beaver Dam Community Library. Lois Ehlert's continued commitment to nurturing creativity, learning, and discovery in children is evident in the way she describes her own work: "The ideas for my books develop as slowly as seeds I plant in early spring. Ideas and seeds both have to be nurtured to grow."

Exploring the Books of Lois Ehlert: Activities for Any Time

In addition to the activities suggested for each of the Lois Ehlert titles featured in this book, you can use the following techniques to build on children's understanding of the author's work, enrich their literature experiences, and enhance your author study as a whole.

Cut-Paper Collage

The technique Lois Ehlert uses most often in her artwork is collage: gluing bits of paper, fabric, or objects onto a backing. Ehlert has said that one of the reasons she prefers this technique is that it gives her the opportunity to try out different combinations before committing to a final image. Rather than draw different versions of the same picture numerous times, she can move the pieces around to see how they will look in different positions, then glue them down when the picture looks just right. She also often uses watercolors to paint her own papers for her cut-paper collages: This way she can create her own unique, vibrant colors for her illustrations. Invite children to try Ehlert's technique with their own collages!

1. Cover a large table with newspapers. Set out plain white paper (absorbent watercolor paper works best), watercolor paints, brushes, cups of water, scissors, and glue.

2. Invite children to create their own colored papers for their collages. They can experiment with mixing and layering different colors to make their own special shades.

3. When the papers have dried, invite children to cut out shapes for their collages. They might like to stick with Ehlert's focus on nature and create items such as leaves or flowers. If they prefer, children can also create abstract collages using any shapes they choose.

4. Provide children with plain white paper for backing, and encourage them to move their shapes around the paper to try out different positions and combinations before gluing them down.

5. When children's work is complete, you can display it on a bulletin board, or you might attach the collages side by side to make a colorful banner to border your classroom.

For the Love of Nature

Lois Ehlert's books are infused with her love of nature. From plants and animals to acorns and snowballs, she finds beauty and fascination in the simple things that make up the natural landscape of the world. Use the author's work to enhance children's appreciation of the beauty in nature that surrounds them every day.

◎ As you explore each book, encourage children to point out natural items they find particularly appealing: It might be a leaf, a flower, or a butterfly. What do they like about these things? What makes them beautiful or special?

◎ Encourage children to be on the lookout, both in and out of school, for details of nature. Invite them to collect any special items they see and bring them in to class—for instance, a bird's feather, a fallen leaf, an unusual stone, or a beautiful wildflower. (Be sure children understand which items are safe to collect and which they should not disturb, such as a bird's nest or a neighbor's rose garden.)

◎ Set aside space for a "nature museum" in your science center for children to display their items. They can create "plaques" on index cards, naming the item and telling where they found it. Encourage children to explore the museum on a regular basis, noting textures, colors, and shapes. Invite children to discuss the items they contributed with the group, telling what they like about them and what makes them beautiful.

Creativity Corner

When Lois Ehlert was a child, she had her own art studio. It was nothing but a small folding table with leftover supplies from her parents' creative projects, but it was all her own. She also emphasizes the unusual nature of the art materials she was provided with: fabric scraps and buttons from her mother's sewing, wood scraps from her father's carpentry, and other items that people might have thrown away. Set up a Creativity Corner in your classroom for children to use during choice time. In addition to traditional art materials such as paper and paints, keep a supply of recyclable items and scraps left over from other projects. Encourage children to be free with the materials, cutting, crumpling, pasting, and combining them to make new creations. Emphasize that once children enter the corner, it is time to let their imagination take over.

Cycles and Changes

Life cycles and seasonal changes are recurring themes in Lois Ehlert's books. *Red Leaf, Yellow Leaf* explores the growth of a tree and the changes it goes through with each season. *Planting a Rainbow* and *Growing Vegetable Soup* explore the cyclical process of plant growth. *Waiting for Wings* describes the life cycle of a butterfly. Even *Feathers for Lunch* features an animal perfect for life cycle explorations: birds.

As children explore the order of the seasons and the life cycles of plants and animals, have them create sequencing puzzles for each concept. Provide children with oblong strips of tagboard divided into several frames. Have children illustrate each life cycle stage (for instance, egg, caterpillar, chrysalis, butterfly) or each seasonal change (for instance, a tree with snow, colored leaves, buds, then flowers) in sequential frames. Then have them cut the frames apart, trade puzzles with a partner, and try to put the pictures back in order. You can store children's puzzles in self-sealing bags to use over and over again.

Connections to the Language Arts Standards

The activities in this book are designed to support you in meeting the following standards outlined by the Mid-continent Research for Education and Learning (MCREL), an organization that collects and synthesizes national and state K–12 curriculum standards.

Language Arts

Uses the general skills and strategies of the reading process:

- Knows that print and written symbols convey meaning and represent spoken language
- Understands that illustrations and pictures convey meaning
- Knows that print appears in different forms (for example, labels, letters, storybooks) and serves different purposes (for example, to inform)
- Predicts story events or outcomes, using illustrations and prior knowledge as a guide
- Uses emergent reading skills to "read" a story (gathers meaning from words and pictures)
- Knows that books have titles, authors, and often illustrators
- Uses visual and verbal cues, including pictures, to comprehend new words and stories

Uses the general skills and strategies of the writing process:

- Knows that writing, including pictures, letters, and words, communicates meaning and information
- Uses drawings to express thoughts, feelings, and ideas
- Dictates stories, poems, and personal narratives
- Uses emergent writing skills to write for a variety of purposes (for example, to make lists, to send messages, to write stories) and to write in a variety of forms (for example, journals, sign-in sheets, name cards, cards with words and pictures)
- Uses writing tools and materials (for example, pencils, crayons, chalk, markers, rubber stamps, computers, paper, cardboard, chalkboard)

Uses listening and speaking strategies for different purposes:

- Uses new vocabulary to describe feelings, thoughts, experiences, and observations
- Uses descriptive language (for example, color words; size words, such as bigger, smaller; shape words)
- Answers simple questions
- Retells a story with attention to the sequence of main events

Source: *Content Knowledge: A Compendium of Standards and Benchmarks for K–12 Education* (4th ed.). Mid-continent Research for Education and Learning, 2004.

Red Leaf, Yellow Leaf

(HARCOURT BRACE, 1991)

In simple, engaging text, this book shows how a tree makes its journey from the woods to the nursery to a child's backyard. Once the tree is planted, the child watches it grow and change with each season. As the story ends, we learn that the best time to look at the tree is in the fall—and a dazzling collage of color shows us why.

Concepts and Themes

▲ ▲ ▲ ▲ ▲ ▲

- ☼ seasons
- ☼ autumn
- ☼ trees and leaves
- ☼ growth and change

Before Reading

Activate children's prior knowledge about trees by asking whether they have any trees in their yards or have seen them on the streets of their neighborhood. Ask:

* Can you see trees where you live? Where?
* How do you think the trees got there? Did someone plant them?

Then invite children to think about seasonal changes by asking:

* Do trees look different in the summer from the way they look in the winter? What changes can you see?
* How do trees look in the fall? What happens to the leaves?

Show children the book cover, and read the title aloud. Can children predict which season is the author's favorite?

After Reading

Talk with children about the journey the child's tree took as it grew. Ask:

* From the story, what do you think a nursery is?
* How did the tree get from the nursery to the child's backyard?
* How did the tree change as it grew? How did it look in each season?

Then discuss the feelings the child shares about her tree. Invite children to share their own feelings about trees as well. Ask:

* How do you think this child feels about her tree? Why do you think she loves it so much?
* What is your favorite thing about trees? In which season do you think they look best?

Talk with children about some of the things trees do: give us shade, make homes for birds—and even give children a good place to climb!

A Tree for All Seasons

(Art and Science)

Children can "grow" a tree in the classroom and help it change along with the seasons.

1. Provide a large sheet of brown craft paper, and invite children to help you draw the outline of a bare tree (trunk and branches) and cut it out. Place the tree at eye level on a bulletin board or wall of your classroom.

2. Throughout the year, have children look out the window or take a short walk outside to observe what the trees look like. Are there leaves or buds? Snow and ice? What colors can children see?

3. As the trees outside change with each season, have children add different collage materials to their classroom tree. For instance, in winter they might cut icicles from white paper and hang them from the branches. In fall, children can cut leaf shapes from red, yellow, orange, and brown construction paper to add to their tree. In spring they might add green leaves and flower buds.

4. Encourage children to compare the trees outside with their classroom tree on a regular basis.

What's in a Leaf? (Science)

With this experiment, children learn that fall colors can be hidden in leaves all year round.

1. Collect green leaves from a few different kinds of trees and place them in separate clear jars. (Help children sort the leaves to make sure they do not place leaves from different trees in the same jar.) You might choose to do this experiment several times throughout the year. The hidden reds and yellows may be very faint in September, but by the next month they can be dazzling!

2. Help children use a fork to grind up the leaves in each jar. Add nail polish remover (with acetone) to each jar until it is about a quarter full. Be sure to supervise very closely for safety.

3. Let the mixture sit for several hours. During this time, help children cut long strips from coffee filters and tape the ends to the middle of a pencil. Place the pencils across the jar openings so that the strip dips into the mixture.

4. Check the filters several hours later (or the next day). What colors do children see on the strips?

Leafy Sort and Graph (Math)

Collect, sort, and graph to see which types of leaves are most common in your area.

1. If possible, go on a nature walk with children to collect leaves from different trees. Alternatively, you can collect the leaves yourself and bring them in to class.

2. Mix up all the leaves and invite children to sort them using criteria such as size, shape, and color.

3. As children sort, help them create graphs on chart paper to show their findings. For instance, you might create a color graph with column headings labeled "Red," "Yellow," and "Green." Have children place a tick mark in the appropriate column for each leaf they sort. You can create different graphs to show color and shape.

4. When the graphs are complete, discuss the results. Did children find more green leaves or more leaves of different colors? Which shape was the most and least common? Help children determine whether more trees in your area have large leaves or smaller leaves.

Tree Terms (Language Arts)

Help children learn more about trees by collecting words and finding definitions.

1. Look through the book with children to find words relating to trees. Some they might find are *seeds, sprouts, roots, trunk,* and *leaves.* (The informational section in the back of the book contains additional words such as *sap, buds, flowers,* and *bark.*)

2. Help children find more information on each "tree term." You can start by looking in the back of the book, and extend your research to library books or the Internet.

3. Use the information you find to make a class picture dictionary about trees. Write a word on each page, let children draw a picture, and help them write or dictate a definition or a fact they learned.

4. You might also have children create a drawing of a tree, label its various parts with the words they learned, and use it as a cover. Bind the pages together, and add the book to your classroom library.

Prints and Rubbings Mural (Art)

Children can create a beautiful and unique mural with nature as their canvas.

1. Go outside with children to collect a variety of leaves. They can also collect fallen twigs and small branches, if available.

2. Back in the classroom, set out a large sheet of craft paper, tempera paints, brushes, paper, and crayons. To make rubbings, children can lay a leaf or twig under the paper and rub the surface with the side of a crayon. To make prints, have them coat the tops of the leaves with a layer of paint, then gently press on the paper to make an impression.

3. You might create two separate murals: one for prints and rubbings and one for the natural materials they were made from. Simply have children glue the leaves and twigs to a separate sheet of craft paper when they are finished using them.

4. You can hang the murals side by side for children to compare. Can they guess which natural item was used to make each rubbing or print?

Count-a-Leaf (Math)

Use the reproducible patterns on page 13 to create a game that helps children practice counting skills.

1. Make several copies of the activity sheet, one for each child. Have children work in small groups to create and play the game.

2. Help children cut the sheet along the dashed line to separate the tree from the leaf patterns. (Children can color in their trees and leaves if they wish.) Each player gets a tree. All players cut apart their leaves and place them in a center pile.

3. Provide a number cube for each group. Players take turns rolling the number cube and adding that number of leaves to their tree. When there are no more leaves in the pile, players count the leaves on their trees. The player with the most leaves wins the game.

4. Children can also play a variation to practice subtraction. Have children start by dividing the leaves evenly among players and placing them on their trees. Players roll the number cube to see how many leaves to remove on each turn. The first player to empty his or her tree wins the game.

Count-a-Leaf

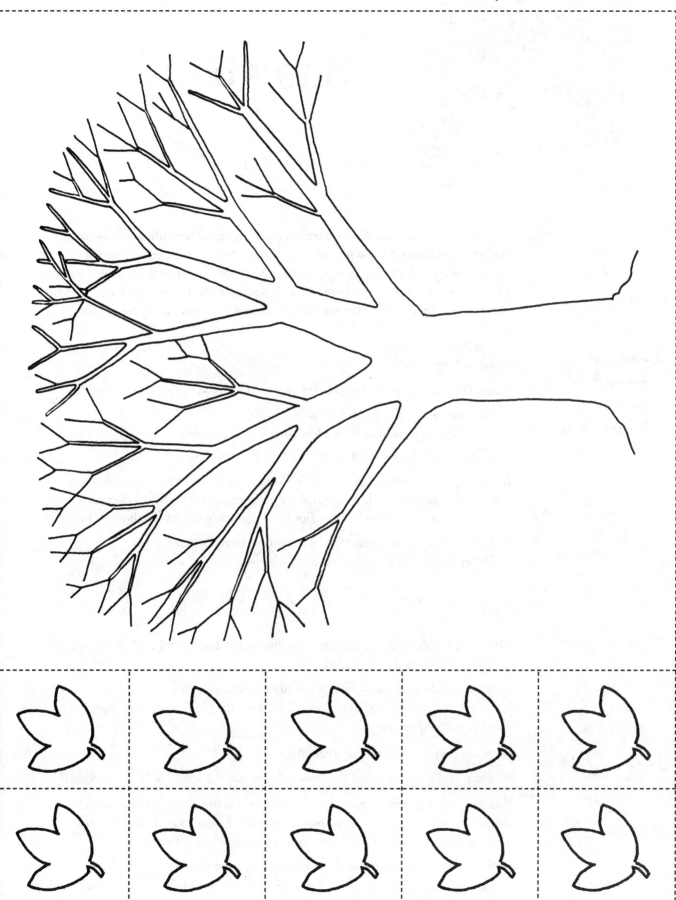

Snowballs

(HARCOURT BRACE, 1995)

Concepts and Themes

▲▲▲▲▲▲

* ☼ winter
* ☼ weather
* ☼ snow
* ☼ changes in matter

Snowballs is a collection of dazzling collages combined with a simple story about building a snow family. The narrator has been preparing for the snowstorm by collecting a sack of "good stuff." Each member of the snow family gets to wear different items from the sack: special hats, buttons, ribbons, even a necktie. The story ends as the sun comes out and the snow family melts away.

Before Reading

Activate children's prior knowledge about snow. Ask:

* ✳ At what time of year does it snow?
* ✳ What does snow look like? How does it feel and taste?
* ✳ What kinds of activities do you like to do in the snow?

If you live in a warm climate, ask children if they have ever visited a place where it snowed. Encourage children to share their experiences. Show them the cover of the book and ask them to predict what the story might be about. Then ask:

* ✳ Have you ever made snowballs or built a snow person?
* ✳ What happened to the snow when the weather got warmer?

After Reading

Talk with children about the snow people in the book, and look at the spread of "good stuff" in the back. Ask:

* ✳ What made each snow family member unique?
* ✳ Can you find each collage material in the story? What was the most surprising item you saw?

Next, discuss the end of the story. Ask:

* ✳ Were you surprised that the snow people melted away? Why or why not?

You may want to paraphrase the "snow info" on the last two pages to help children understand how snow forms. They will also enjoy looking at the photographs of children building their own snow people. Ask:

* ✳ What kinds of props did these children use for their snow people?
* ✳ Have you ever built a snow creature? How did it compare to the ones shown in the book?

My Snow Family (Art)

Invite children to try a snowy twist on a family portrait. How might their own families look made out of snow?

1. Provide children with a supply of precut white paper circles of several different sizes. Set out collage materials such as yarn and buttons, and natural materials such as leaves, twigs, and small pinecones.

2. Invite children to glue the white paper "snowballs" to a sheet of construction paper to build their snow family. They can use small, medium, and large circles to create a snow person representing each family member. Encourage children to include snow pets as well!

3. Next, have children use the collage materials to add features. They might use buttons for eyes, twigs for arms, and yarn for hair or a scarf. Encourage children to be creative; as they saw in the book, scrap materials can be used in many interesting ways.

4. Help children label their completed portraits with each family member's name.

Breaking the Ice (Science)

What happens to ice and snow when it meets the warm sun? Find out!

1. Gather ice cubes and place them in plastic bowls. Invite children to place the bowls in various spots in the classroom, such as on a windowsill, under a warm lamp, and away from the light.

2. Invite children to predict what will happen to the ice cubes. Which one do they think will melt first? Keep a log with children to track the process. You might have them draw pictures of what each ice cube looks like at various intervals.

3. When all the ice cubes have melted, list the locations in order from "melted first" to "melted last." How did light and heat affect the melting speed?

To introduce the three forms water can take, you might try an additional ice cube experiment:

◎ Tell children they can make ice cubes "fly." They will probably be very surprised! Place a few ice cubes in a teakettle or electric hot pot (be sure to supervise closely for safety).

◎ When you turn on the heat, the ice will first melt into water and then become steam—making the ice cubes "fly" out of the pot. Children have just observed all three forms of water: solid, liquid, and gas.

Good Stuff (Art)

Why not collect your own sack of "good stuff" for a snowy day? The narrator of *Snowballs* collected leaves, seashells, branches, buttons, and even bottle caps. As winter approaches, go on scavenger hunts both in the classroom and outdoors to look for materials to enhance a snow sculpture. When the snow arrives, get out your sack and make a special creation! If you live in an area where it does not snow, you might create a giant snowman out of large circles of craft paper. Add your "good stuff" and hang your creation on a wall of the classroom.

Winter Word Wall (Language Arts)

Create a winter-themed word wall for language activities.

1. First, help children make paper snowflakes. Distribute precut circles of white paper and help children fold them in half to make a semicircle, then in half again to make a triangle. Have children use scissors to cut pieces out of each edge of the triangle. When they unfold the paper, they will see a snowflake shape.

2. Next, invite children to look through the book for words associated with winter. Some they might find are: *snow, snowball, slush,* and *melting.* Write these words on snowflakes.

3. Then help children brainstorm more winter words, such as *cold, frost, blizzard, ice,* and *chilly.* Write these on additional snowflakes.

4. You can post the snowflakes on a bulletin board to create a snowstorm of winter words. Use the words to create a winter class poem or story.

Frosty Patterns (Science)

Let children see firsthand with this simple activity how frost forms. Help children dip several clear glass jars or containers quickly into a tub of water (supervise closely for safety). Immediately place the glasses either in a freezer or outside on a very cold day. Allow them to chill for an hour or more, until they become frosty. Set out paper, crayons, and magnifiers. Distribute the glasses and invite children to examine them with the magnifiers. What do they see? (They will see tiny frost crystals that look like snowflakes.) Encourage children to draw the patterns they see—and to work fast before the frost melts! When they are finished, invite children to compare their patterns. They will see that just like snowflakes, no two frost patterns are exactly alike.

No-Cook Snowball Treats (Cooking)

Why not make a batch of edible snowballs for a wintertime snack? This recipe is easy, fun, and doesn't require an oven. Let children help measure and stir the ingredients. To incorporate literacy skills, you may want to write the recipe on chart paper and add rebus illustrations. Invite children to read along as you follow each step.

Snowball Treats

6 oz. cream cheese, softened
5 cups powdered sugar
1/2 teaspoon vanilla
1 bag shredded coconut flakes

1. In a large bowl, combine sugar and cream cheese. Stir well.
2. Add the vanilla. Stir again.
3. Roll the mixture into balls. Use about a teaspoon of the mixture for each ball.
4. Spread the coconut flakes on a cookie sheet. Roll each ball in the flakes until it is covered.
5. Refrigerate until well chilled.
6. Enjoy the yummy blizzard!

Variation: Children might also enjoy building snow people out of their snowballs. They can stack the balls to make snowmen and add features such as raisins for eyes and licorice whips for hair. As with any food-related activity, be sure to check for allergies before children eat their treats.

Snowman Button Math (Math)

Use the snowman pattern on page 18 to help children practice counting skills. Make one copy of the pattern for each child. Invite children to color in their snowmen if they wish (but make sure they do not add features such as buttons or eyes). Provide children with a supply of small buttons. Then share math stories that children can act out with the buttons. To get started, see the examples below.

- **Addition:** The snowman had two button eyes on his head. He had three buttons on his middle. He had two buttons on the bottom. How many buttons did he have all together?

- **Subtraction:** The snowman had two button eyes on his head. He had three more buttons down his middle, but then one fell off. How many buttons were left on the snowman?

- **Logical Thinking:** The snowman had six buttons all together. He had the same amount of buttons on the top, middle, and bottom. How many buttons did he have on each part?

Snowman Button Math

Snowman
Button Math

Planting a Rainbow

Planting a Rainbow by Lois Ehlert

(HARCOURT, 1988)

In this cyclical story, a child describes the garden of color she plants with her mother every year. In the fall, the seeds and bulbs are planted. They wait all winter long for spring to warm the soil, and then the garden bursts into bloom. Summer is spent picking the different-colored flowers. And when summer is over, the planting can begin anew!

Concepts and Themes

* seasons
* growth
* flowers and plants
* colors

Before Reading

Find out what children know about flowers and plants. Ask:

* Do you have any plants in your home or in your yard? Do you help take care of them? How?
* What are some things that plants and flowers need to grow?
* Do you know the names of any flowers? Can you describe what your favorite flower looks like? What color is it?

Show children the cover of the book and invite them to predict what it might be about. Next, invite children to share any experiences they may have had with gardens or gardening. Ask:

* Have you ever helped to grow a garden or planted a seed in the ground? How did you do it? What happened next?
* Have you ever seen a garden in bloom? What did it look like? What colors did you see?

After Reading

Page through the "rainbow" section of the book again, encouraging children to look at the different flowers and name each color. You might also like to read aloud the labels to teach children the name of each flower. Ask:

* Have you ever seen any of the flowers shown in the book? Where?
* Which color and flower do you like best? Why?

Then discuss the growth cycle with children. Invite them to retell the sequence. Ask:

* In what season did the girl and her mother plant the seeds?
* In what season did the garden start to grow?
* What do you think the girl and her mother will do when summer is over?

How Does Our Garden Grow? (Science)

Invite children to create their own garden to see what sprouts!

1. Brainstorm with children a list of things they would like to plant in a classroom garden. Invite them to suggest different kinds of seeds, such as apple seeds, fruit pits, beans, or flower seeds.

2. Then invite children to suggest other types of things they might plant. Encourage them to be creative: Any small object can be buried in soil, from a penny to a toy car. Accept all suggestions.

3. Fill a window box with soil and let children plant the items they suggested. Help them make markers from craft sticks. They can attach a small sticky note to each stick and label it with the type of seed or object they planted.

4. Invite children to look at the markers and predict which items will sprout and which will not. Keep your garden in a sunny spot and water it regularly. Encourage children to check the garden on a regular basis to see what grows. How close were their predictions?

Seed and Flower Sort (Math)

Invite children to sort seeds and flowers by various characteristics.

1. Collect a variety of seeds (such as sunflower, apple, grape, cherry pits, acorns, beans, and popcorn kernels) and a variety of flowers (such as daisies, carnations, and wildflowers).

2. Look at the seeds with children. Work together to create a list of attributes, such as *brown, small, oval,* and *round.* Do the same for the flowers, using words such as *petals, leaves, thorns,* and *red.* Write each attribute word on an index card. Keep the seed attribute cards separate from the flower attribute cards.

3. Set out two circles of yarn or two hula hoops on the floor, overlapping them to create a Venn diagram. To sort seeds, place a seed attribute card above each circle. Help children read the labels and sort the seeds accordingly. For instance, if the attributes chosen were *brown* and *oval,* all brown seeds would go in one circle, all oval seeds would go in the other circle, and all brown, oval seeds would go in the center section. All other seeds would be placed outside the diagram. Repeat using different attribute cards.

4. Next, have children sort flowers by choosing two flower attribute cards to place above the circles. Repeat the activity several times, using a different combination of attributes each time.

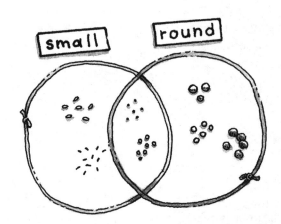

Sunlight Science (Science)

With this experiment, children learn just how important sunlight is to plants.

1. Work with the class or with small groups of children to plant a seed in a small pot (a lima bean will work well). Water the soil until the seed begins to sprout.

2. Once the seed has sprouted, help children cut a large hole at one end of a shoe box lid. Place the plant inside the box away from the hole, close the lid, and place the box on a windowsill or near another light source.

3. Ask children to predict what will happen to the plant. What would plants do without sunshine? Have children lift the lid and water their plant on a regular basis, replacing the lid each time.

4. Children can keep a plant journal and draw pictures of what is happening to the plant at various intervals. Eventually, they will see that the plant grows in the direction of the light. If the plant grows big enough, children might even see it grow right out of the hole in the shoe box!

Birthday Bouquet Graph (Math)

Did you know that each birth month has a special flower? Invite children to create a graph of their birth months and the flowers associated with them.

1. To begin, write the birth months and flowers listed at right on a sheet of chart paper.

2. Next, create a simple chart with 12 columns. Write the names of the flowers as headings and include a picture of each flower if possible.

3. Provide children with sticky notes labeled with their names. Invite them to find their birth month on the list, then place their name under the appropriate flower on the graph.

4. When the graph is complete, work with children to discuss and interpret the results. For instance, which flower has the most names? With this information, can children tell which month has the most birthdays? Are there more names under the orchid or the daffodil? Were more children born in December or March?

5. You might like to extend the activity by having groups of children with the same birth month work together to create a drawing or painting of their flower. Have children label their work with the name of the month. Display the flowers on a bulletin board for a beautiful birthday bouquet!

January ✿ Carnation
February ✿ Iris
March ✿ Daffodil
April ✿ Daisy
May ✿ Lily of the Valley
June ✿ Rose
July ✿ Sunflower
August ✿ Gladiolus
September ✿ Aster
October ✿ Snapdragon
November ✿ Chrysanthemum
December ✿ Orchid

Additional Resources

Alison's Zinnia
by Anita Lobel
(Greenwillow, 1990)

An alphabet chain is created as children give flowers that begin with the first letter of their names to a recipient whose name begins with the next letter in the alphabet. When Zena gives a Zinnia back to Alison, the circle is complete!

Flower Garden
by Eve Bunting
(Harcourt, 1994)

Through rhyming text and lush illustrations, this story shows that you don't need a backyard to grow beautiful flowers. Children will enjoy seeing a little girl plant a garden for her mother in a window high above the city streets.

Jack's Garden
by Henry Cole
(Scott Foresman, 1995)

In a cumulative story that follows the pattern of "This Is the House That Jack Built," children trace the growth of a little boy's garden—from tilling the soil to enjoying the blossoms.

The Tiny Seed
by Eric Carle
(Simon & Schuster, 1987)

This classic tells the story of a seed that travels from one place to another until it settles into the earth to grow—and over time, the tiny seed becomes a giant flower.

Rainbow Garden Banner (Language Arts and Math)

Use the reproducible activity sheet on page 23 to "plant" your own rainbow right in the classroom!

1. Make one copy of the activity sheet for each child and cut it out along the dashed lines. Divide the class into six groups and assign each group a color: red, orange, yellow, green, blue, or purple.

2. Invite children to choose a flower or plant that is their assigned color. They might choose one from the book or look through seed and gardening catalogs to find a different one. Encourage each child in the group to choose a different flower or plant.

3. Have children use crayons to draw a picture of their flower "growing" out of the grass. Make sure they use the correct color crayon for their flower.

4. Help children fill in the blanks to complete the poem. They can write or dictate the color on the first line and the name of the flower or plant on the second line.

5. When children have finished, put the sheets in rainbow color order. Attach the sheets side by side on a wall of the classroom to create a garden banner. Encourage children to share their own work and learn the names and colors of all the flowers in the garden.

○ ○ ○ ○ ○ ○ ○

Name _____

I planted something _____ ,

and I watched it grow.

Now my _____

is part of our garden rainbow!

Growing Vegetable Soup

(HARCOURT, 1987)

Concepts and Themes

▲▲▲▲▲▲

✳ **planting and growth**

✳ **vegetables**

✳ **food and cooking**

✳ **working together**

When a child and her father want vegetable soup, they don't go to the supermarket—they grow the ingredients themselves. They work together to plant the seeds and sprouts, water the soil, and pull the weeds. Finally it is time to pick the vegetables, take them home, and put them in a pot. Their recipe takes a lot of time and hard work—but it makes the best soup ever!

Before Reading

Activate children's prior knowledge about vegetables. Ask:

✳ Do you like to eat vegetables? What are some names of different vegetables? Which is your favorite?

✳ Have you ever eaten vegetable soup? How did it taste? Did you like it? What kinds of vegetables were in the soup?

Then show children the cover of the book and read the title. Invite children to discuss what the title might mean. Ask:

✳ How could you grow vegetable soup? What might happen if you planted a can of soup in the ground?

✳ Where do you think the vegetables in soup come from?

After Reading

Invite children to retell the story and build sequencing skills. Ask:

✳ What was the first step in growing the vegetable soup? What did the girl and her father do next? After that?

✳ It took a lot of work to make soup this way. Why do you think they grew the ingredients themselves, instead of going to the store to buy soup?

✳ Do you think it would be more fun to make soup from scratch or to buy it in a can? Why?

Page through the book again and invite children to look closely at the pictures. How many gardening tools and vegetables can they name? Read the labels to children as you point to each picture. Then talk about how different vegetables grow. Ask:

✳ Why do you think the girl picked some vegetables but had to dig others up from the ground? Which vegetables do you think grow above the ground? Which grow underneath?

Group Soup! (Cooking)

Reinforce the concepts of teamwork and cooperation by helping children make a collaborative pot of favorite-vegetable soup.

1. Talk with children about their favorite vegetables and list them on the board. How can children work together to make a soup that will include everyone's favorite? Send home a note to family members asking them to bring in their child's favorite vegetable. Let children describe the vegetable they brought.

2. Work with children to wash and cut the vegetables into bite-size pieces. Softer vegetables (such as mushrooms) can be cut with a plastic knife.

3. Pour a few cans of vegetable broth into a large pot and bring to a boil. Let children add the vegetables, supervising closely for safety. Turn down the heat and simmer until the vegetables are tender, about 10–15 minutes. Let the soup cool and enjoy! (As with any food activity, be sure to check for food allergies first.)

4. As children eat, encourage them to talk about how it felt to work together. Would the soup have been as good if everyone brought the same vegetable? They might find that teamwork makes a recipe even tastier!

5. For an extension that incorporates literacy skills, help children list the ingredients and the steps they used to make the soup. They can write or dictate the recipe on a large index card and add illustrations. Invite them to take the recipe cards home and make the soup with their families.

Veggie Vision Print Art (Art)

Invite children to use vegetables to make unique print collages.

1. Gather a variety of vegetables, such as potatoes, carrots, celery, radishes, peppers, and broccoli. Cut the vegetables in half or into smaller pieces to make cross-sections.

2. Provide children with white construction paper and shallow dishes of tempera paint. Show them how to dip the vegetable lightly into the paint, then gently press on the paper to make a print.

3. Let children make print collages using any combination of colors and vegetables they choose. Encourage them to be creative— in addition to creating prints, they might use a flower of broccoli or the leaves on a celery stalk as a paintbrush!

4. When dry, display children's work at eye level on a bulletin board or wall of the classroom. Set the vegetables out on a table and challenge children to guess which vegetable made each print.

How Do Plants Eat? (Science)

With this simple experiment, children learn how roots and stems "feed" plants the water they need to grow.

1. Help children cut the ends off a few celery stalks, about an inch from the bottom. Place each stalk in a clear jar filled with about three inches of water. Add a few drops of food coloring to the water, using a different color for each jar.

2. Ask children what they think will happen to the celery. Check the stalks every few hours for signs of change. Soon children will see that the leaves have turned color. How did it happen?

3. Take the stalks out of the jars and examine them with children. Scrape the surface of the stalk so they can see the colored tubes, and then cut the stalk in half. What do children see? Talk with them about how roots and stems help pull water up to feed all the parts of a plant.

4. For a fun variation, try splitting a stalk of celery in half vertically, but without cutting all the way to the top (so that the leaves stay intact). Place one half of the stalk in a jar of blue water and the other half in red water. What color will the leaves turn? (purple)

This Is the Way We Grow Our Food (Music and Dramatic Play)

Invite children to explore what gardeners do.

1. Look through the book with children for different gardening tools. Some they might find are a rake, hoe, shovel, trowel, watering can, and gloves. How do children think these tools are used?

2. Work with children to explore the actions involved in growing a vegetable garden, such as digging soil, planting seeds, watering sprouts, pulling weeds, and harvesting the plants. Invite them to pantomime using gardening tools to do these actions.

3. When children have a repertoire of gardening movements, teach them a variation on the popular chant "This Is the Way We Wash Our Clothes":

   This is the way we dig the soil, dig the soil, dig the soil.
   This is the way we dig the soil, so early in the morning.

   Sing the song as children act out the movement. Then substitute the words *dig the soil* with different phrases, such as *plant the seeds*, or *pull the weeds*. Sing the song several times as children act out each step.

4. If possible, add play gardening tools to your dramatic play center or sand table. Let children use the tools to plant an imaginary garden.

Seeded or Seedless? (Math and Science)

Gather a variety of produce, such as lettuce, broccoli, celery, carrots, cauliflower, tomatoes, peppers, and cucumbers. As you show children each vegetable, invite them to predict whether or not it will have seeds inside. Then cut the vegetables open and find out! Make a simple T-chart labeled "Seeded" and "Seedless." As you explore each vegetable, write it in the appropriate column. How close were children's predictions? Were there any surprises?

When your chart is complete, you can give children another surprise by explaining the definition of a fruit: It's the part of the plant that contains the seed. Children may be very surprised to find out that the "vegetables" in the "Seeded" column are technically fruits!

Above and Below (Science)

Invite children to explore which vegetables grow above and which grow below the ground.

1. Give children each a sheet of paper and have them fold it in half. Help them label the top half of the sheet "Above" and the bottom half "Below."

2. Provide children with produce catalogs or supermarket flyers with pictures of vegetables. Invite children to cut out any vegetable pictures that appeal to them. Do they think the vegetable grows above the ground or underground? Have them place their pictures on the appropriate part of the paper to show their predictions (but without gluing the pictures down).

3. Next, help children check their predictions by doing research in reference books or on the Internet. Were their guesses correct?

4. As children find information, have them move their pictures to the appropriate half of the paper and glue them down. Help them label each picture with the name of the vegetable.

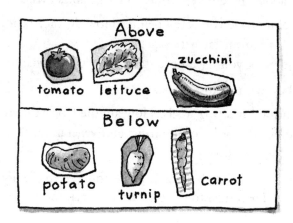

Additional Resources

How Groundhog's Garden Grew
by Lynne Cherry
(Blue Sky, 2003)

When Groundhog gets caught eating vegetables from Squirrel's garden, Squirrel helps him to grow his own. This charming book contains a wealth of information along with an engaging story.

I Eat Vegetables!
by Hannah Tofts
(Zero to Ten, 2001)

Dazzling photographs and clear labels enhance this lift-the-flap book that lets children take a look inside their favorite veggies.

Tops and Bottoms
by Janet Stevens
(Harcourt, 1995)

This Caldecott Honor book tells the story of a smart rabbit who fools a lazy farmer bear. The rabbit does all the work of planting the crops, and lets the farmer choose to keep the "tops" or "bottoms."

The Ugly Vegetables
by Grace Lin
(Charlesbridge, 1999)

A Chinese-American girl is disappointed when her mother insists on growing "ugly" Chinese vegetables in their garden, instead of the beautiful flowers their neighbors grow. But when the vegetables are used to make a delicious soup, all the neighbors want to try it—and bring beautiful bouquets as thank-yous.

Eating the Alphabet
Fruits & Vegetables from A to Z

◆◆

(H A R C O U R T ,   1 9 8 9)

From *Apple* to *Zucchini*, gorgeous collage paintings bring this innovative alphabet book to life. A variety of both familiar and exotic fruits and vegetables are introduced in alphabetical order, with labels in both uppercase and lowercase letters. The back of the book contains a glossary of information about each food, including its history, where it comes from, and how it is grown.

Concepts and Themes

▲▲▲▲▲▲

☼ **fruits**

☼ **vegetables**

☼ **alphabet**

Before Reading

Show children the front and back covers of the book. Ask:

✳ What foods do you see on the front cover? What do they have in common? (They are all fruits.)

✳ What foods do you see on the back cover? What do they have in common? (They are all vegetables.)

✳ What letter of the alphabet does *strawberry* start with? How about *tomato*?

Next, read the title of the book aloud. Ask:

✳ What do you think it means to "eat the alphabet"?

✳ What is a fruit whose name begins with the letter *a*? How about a vegetable that begins with a *b*?

Continue to invite children to suggest fruits and vegetables that begin with different letters. Which fruits and vegetables do children think they will see in the book?

After Reading

Encourage children to talk about the different fruits and vegetables they saw. Ask:

✳ Which fruits and vegetables have you eaten before? How do they taste?

✳ Which is your favorite fruit? Your favorite vegetable?

✳ What is one food in the book you have never tasted but would like to try?

Next, examine the text labels with children. Ask:

✳ Why do you think each food has two labels? How are the labels different?

✳ What did you notice about the order of the fruits and vegetables? Why might the author have shown them in this order?

You might also like to page through the book and invite children to classify each food as a fruit or a vegetable. Then turn to the glossary to check their guesses.

Fruit and Vegetable Tasting Party (Math)

Invite children to taste-test fruits and vegetables to see which they like best. As with any food-related activity, check for allergies first.

1. Look through the book with children for fruits and vegetables they would like to try. As children choose foods, write them on chart paper to make a shopping list.

2. Gather the fruits and vegetables for tasting. You can ask children's family members to each bring in an item from the list, or, if possible, take children on a field trip to the market.

3. Cut each fruit or vegetable into bite-size pieces for tasting. Place the foods on separate paper plates. Write the name of each food on an index card or sticky note and place it beside the plate.

4. Before children begin tasting, make a taste-test chart on chart paper or tagboard. List the foods down the left side and label three columns across the top: "Like," "Don't Like," "Not Sure."

5. Now it's time to eat! Invite children to try each food and place a tick mark in the column that shows what they thought of it. Encourage children to describe tastes and textures as well. Is it crunchy? Soft? Tangy? Sweet?

6. When all the foods have been tasted, look at the chart together. Which foods did most children like? Which was the least popular? Which foods are children unsure about?

A Is for *Apple* at Alice's Restaurant (Language Arts)

In this restaurant, children serve foods beginning with the letters in their names!

1. Invite children to create menus for their own restaurant. Help them write the letters of their name down the left side of a sheet of paper, acrostic style.

2. Encourage children to think of a food they would like to serve in their restaurant that begins with each letter of their name—for instance, Carlo might serve *Cookies, Applesauce, Rice, Lemonade,* and *Oatmeal.*

3. Have children draw a picture of each food next to the letter. They can write or dictate the name of the food next to the picture, and even add a price.

4. When children's menus are complete, invite them to use them for dramatic play. They can take turns being restaurant owners and customers. Encourage children to say the name of the letter as they order from the menu—for instance: "I'll have the *S* for *Spaghetti.*"

Where in the World Are Watermelons From? (Social Studies)

You can use the glossary in the back of the book to map out fruits and vegetables. Post a world map on an eye-level bulletin board. Look through the book with children to find foods they are interested in knowing more about. Where do children think each food comes from? Look it up in the glossary and help them find the area on your map. Children can draw pictures of the fruits and vegetables on small sticky notes and attach them to the map in the appropriate locations. Explain to children that the information in the glossary tells where each food came from originally—the foods may now be grown in many different places.

Alphabet Pretzels (Cooking)

With this recipe, children can eat the alphabet—literally! Write the recipe on chart paper and let children read along as they help measure and mix the ingredients. Children can shape their pretzels into both uppercase and lowercase letters.

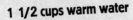

Alphabet Pretzels

1 1/2 cups warm water

1 package yeast

1 teaspoon table salt

1 tablespoon sugar

4 cups flour

1 beaten egg

coarse salt

greased cookie sheets

1. Measure the water into a large mixing bowl. Sprinkle in yeast and stir until it looks soft.
2. Add the salt, sugar, and flour. Mix and knead the dough.
3. Take a piece of dough and make it into the shape of a letter.
4. Lay the pretzels on the cookie sheets, brush the tops with egg, and sprinkle with coarse salt.
5. Bake at 425° for 12 to 15 minutes.
6. Let cool, and enjoy eating the alphabet!

I'm Going on a Picnic (Language Arts)

Try this round-robin game to reinforce listening, memory, and alphabet skills.

1. Gather children in a circle. Start by saying "I'm going on a picnic and I'm bringing *applesauce.*"

2. The child to your left repeats the sentence and adds an item that begins with *b*, for instance: "I'm going on a picnic and I'm bringing *applesauce* and *bean dip.*"

3. The next child continues the alphabet chain—for example, "I'm going on a picnic and I'm bringing *applesauce, bean dip,* and *cake.*"

4. If children cannot think of a food, encourage them to use other words. For example, they might bring their *dog,* or even an *elephant*!

5. Continue until the list gets too long to remember. Then start a new chain beginning with the letter following the one they ended with.

Luscious Letter Place Mats (Language Arts and Art)

Use the reproducible pattern on page 33 to make a set of alphabet place mats for the classroom.

1. Make 26 copies of the page, one for each letter of the alphabet. (You can enlarge the pattern to make bigger place mats.) Assign each child one or more letters, depending on the size of your class, and provide children with the appropriate number of sheets.

2. Invite children to think of a food that begins with their letter and draw it on the plate. Let them know that their food does not have to be a fruit or vegetable, and encourage them to choose a food not included in the book. For instance, your place mat set might include *Animal crackers*, *Burritos*, and *Cornflakes*.

3. For more challenging letters, encourage children to be creative: *Z* might stand for *Zebra cookies*, *X* might stand for *Xylophone cake*, and *Q* might stand for a *Quarter of a pizza pie*! Help children write the letter to complete the poem, and write the name of the food under the plate. When the place mats are complete, you can laminate them or cover them with clear contact paper.

4. Invite children to use the place mats at lunch or snack time. Encourage them to choose a place mat with a different letter each day and read the poem and the name of the food. You might even challenge children to sit at the table in alphabetical order.

Children might also enjoy playing a snack time alphabet guessing game. Have one child say the name of the food on his or her place mat as another child guesses what letter it begins with. The first child can check the place mat to see if the guess was correct.

The letter _____ is hard to beat.

It stands for something good to eat!

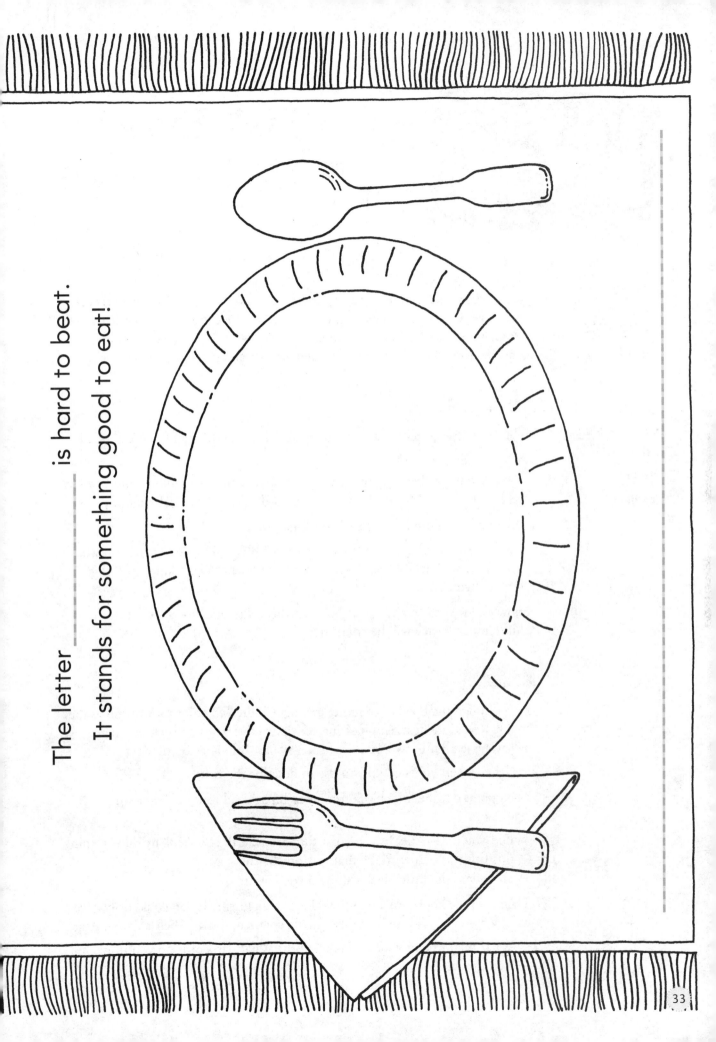

Fish Eyes
A Book You Can Count On

(HARCOURT, 1990)

Concepts and Themes

☼ **numbers and counting**

☼ **fish**

☼ **sea life**

☼ **imagination**

Children take a fantasy journey under the sea with this unique counting book. A succession of fanciful, brightly colored fish with cut-out eyes float through the pages, introducing the numbers 1 to 10. Take a closer look, and you'll also find a camouflaged guide who does simple addition to keep the count going on each page.

Before Reading

Invite children to tell what they know about fish and life under the sea. Ask:

※ Where do fish live?

※ Have you ever been to the ocean or an aquarium? What animals did you see?

※ Have you ever had a fish as a pet? What did it look like? How did it move?

Then invite children to use their imagination. Ask:

※ What might it be like to live underwater? If you lived under the sea, what would you do? How would your life be different? What kinds of things would you see every day?

Show children the cover of the book and read the title aloud. What do children think they will be counting?

After Reading

Page through the book once more, inviting children to point to each fish as they count. Reread the text, emphasizing the descriptive word on each numbered page (one *green* fish, two *jumping* fish, 3 *smiling* fish, and so on). Ask:

※ What other words could you use to describe the fish?

Then point out the little black fish on each page and read the "camouflaged" text. Ask:

※ Did you notice this fish the first time we read the book? Why do you think this fish was harder to see than the other fish?

※ How does the little black fish help you count?

Then read the book's final question aloud to children: "If you could truly have a wish, would you wish to be a fish?" Invite children to share their answers. Ask:

※ What might be nice about being a fish? What parts of it do you think you wouldn't like?

Let's Go Fishing! (Math)

Reinforce sorting skills as children "fish" for colors, patterns, or numerals.

1. Begin by creating a simple fish-shaped template on heavy paper or card stock. Provide children with sheets of colored construction paper. Show them how to place the template on the paper, trace around it, and cut out the fish shape. Have children create fish of different colors, making sure there are several of each type.

2. Create a "pond," using a wading pool, large tub, or cardboard box decorated with blue paper. Attach a paper clip to each fish and place them in the pond. Next, create a fishing pole by tying a string to a wooden dowel and tying a magnet to the end of the string.

3. Invite children to catch fish by touching the magnet to the paper clip on a fish. As they pull fish from the pond, encourage them to sort the fish into piles by color. How many fish of each color did they catch?

Variation: To reinforce pattern recognition, have children draw patterns such as stripes or spots on their fish. Then have children sort the fish they catch by pattern. To reinforce numeral recognition and sequencing skills, have children place ten fish in the pond, numbered from 1 to 10. Challenge them to try to catch the fish in numerical order!

Saltwater Painting (Art and Science)

Invite children to explore the properties of saltwater as they create unique artwork.

1. Begin by talking with children about the differences between freshwater and ocean water. Have children ever tasted water from the ocean? Was it salty? Explain that ocean water contains a great deal of salt.

2. Collect several jars for the saltwater paint. Have children help measure 1/4 cup of warm water, 6 teaspoons of salt, and 3 drops of food coloring into each jar. Mix together to create the paints. Be sure children do not taste the paint!

3. Provide children with white construction paper and paintbrushes. Invite them to use the mixtures to paint pictures of fish or other sea creatures. Encourage them to guess what will happen to the pictures as they dry. Do children think they will look any different?

4. Let the paintings dry, and display. The water will evaporate, but the colored salt will remain—creating beautiful, sparkling pictures.

Fish Wishes (Language Arts)

Why not use the final question in *Fish Eyes* as inspiration for an imaginative, collaborative class book? Write the following sentence stem at the bottom of a sheet of paper: *If I were a fish, I'd wish for _____* . Make one copy of the sheet for each child and invite children to complete the sentence. They can draw a picture showing what they might look like as a fish, and what they would wish for. Work together to design a cover. Then bind the pages together and read the completed book to the class. What kinds of things did your "school of fish" wish for?

How Do Fish Breathe? (Science)

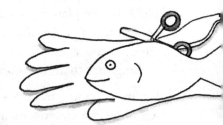

Explore how gills work with this simple activity. Help children draw the outline of a fish on each side of a rubber glove. Cut the fish out—each glove will yield two rubber fish, one from each side. Then help children cut a small slit on each fish to create a "gill." Let children play with the fish in your water table or a large tub of water. They can make the fish "swim" by holding the head and pulling the fish through the water. What happens to the gill as the fish moves? (The gill flap opens and closes as water flows through it.) Compare the gill action of the rubber fish to how real fish use their gills: The gills open and close, helping the fish take air out of the water to breathe.

Camouflage! (Science and Art)

Invite children to explore camouflage and find each other's "secret fish."

1. Begin by discussing camouflage with children. Explain that some fish (and other sea creatures) have colors and textures that make them blend in with their underwater environment. How might camouflage help a fish stay safe?

2. Examine the dark, camouflaged fish in the book with children. How did Ehlert make this fish more difficult to see?

3. Provide children with paints, crayons, construction paper, scissors, and glue. Invite them to create their own pictures that include camouflaged fish. They might use Ehlert's method and create a dark, underwater background. Then they can cut fish shapes out of dark construction paper and paste them in the scene.

4. Children can also explore other methods of camouflage, such as disguising their fish with glitter and collage materials on a colorful "coral reef" background. Invite children to include as many fish in their pictures as they like. When they are finished, have them count the fish they created and write the number on the back of the paper.

5. Invite children to trade pictures with a friend and see how many fish they can find. They can turn the picture over to check their guesses!

Deep Sea Dominoes (Math)

Use the reproducible patterns on page 38 to create a fish-counting domino game.

1. Make as many copies of the dominoes as you like and cut them apart. Invite small groups of children to play the game.

2. Divide the dominoes evenly among players. One player sets out a domino.

3. The next player counts the fish and tries to make a match with one side of one of his or her dominoes. If a match can be made, the domino is placed next to the matching square.

4. Players continue making matches and setting out dominoes to form a chain. Play continues until all possible matches have been made.

Variations: You can also use the dominoes for different counting and number-matching activities:

◎ Write plus (+), minus (−), and equal (=) signs on index cards. Invite children to cut the dominoes in half and use them to make number sentences—for instance: 2 fish + 4 fish = 6 fish.

◎ The dominoes can also be divided in half and used to play concentration. For each pair of children, create two matching sets of cards, each with the numbers 1 to 10. Have children put all the cards together, mix them up, and turn them facedown. They can then take turns turning over two cards at a time until they have matched each card with its partner.

Additional Resources

Big Al
by Andrew Clements
(Aladdin, 1997)

Big Al is a fierce-looking fish who has a hard time finding a friend—the little fish are all afraid of him. But when Al gets the opportunity to save the day, the fish realize that the true worth of a friend lies in the way one acts, not the way one looks.

A Fish Out of Water
by Helen Palmer
(Random House, 1961)

What happens if you feed a pet fish too much? This classic favorite details the hilarious results as a little fish outgrows its bowl, a vase, and even the bathtub!

Pattern Fish
by Trudy Harris
(Millbrook, 2000)

Rhyming text introduces a variety of cartoon fish that inhabit a world of patterns in this innovative concept book. Children will enjoy finding the patterns in the captivating illustrations, which become more and more complex as the story moves along.

Swimmy
by Leo Lionni
(Pantheon, 1963)

This classic story tells the tale of a little fish who helps his friends by teaching them a unique method of camouflage.

Deep Sea Dominoes

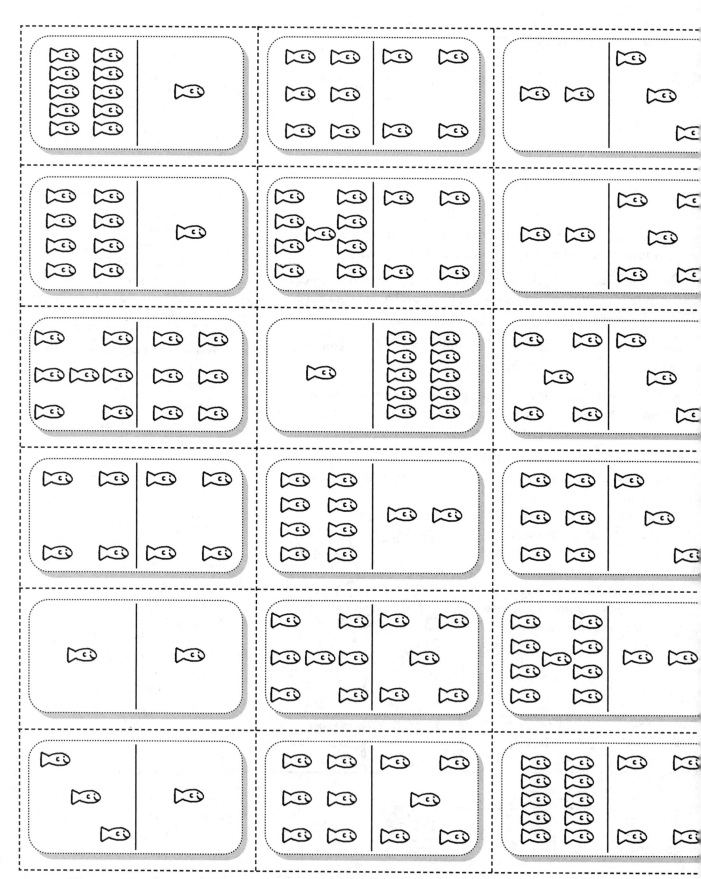

Waiting for Wings

(HARCOURT, 2001)

Celebrating the metamorphosis from egg to butterfly, this beautiful book unfolds in gentle, rhyming text and glorious collages. Partial pages create a book-within-a-book as the life cycle progresses against a lush garden backdrop. As the story ends, the life cycle comes full circle—it is time for the full-grown butterflies to lay new eggs.

Concepts and Themes

- ✳ life cycle
- ✳ butterflies
- ✳ growth and change

Before Reading

Find out what children already know about the butterfly life cycle by asking:

* What do you know about caterpillars? Have you ever seen a caterpillar? What was it doing?
* How do caterpillars change as they grow?
* Have you ever seen a butterfly? What do butterflies look like? How do they move?
* Do butterflies look different when they are born from when they are adults?

Show children the cover of the book and read the title aloud. Ask:

* What do you think "waiting for wings" means? Who do you think is waiting for them?

After Reading

Invite children to retell the sequence of the story. Ask:

* What did the butterflies start out as? What hatched out of the eggs?
* What did the caterpillars build for themselves? What happened inside the cases? What happened when the cases opened?
* What did the butterflies do last? What do you think will happen after the new eggs are laid?

Then invite children to relate the story to their own experience. Point out all the changes the butterflies went through as they grew. Ask:

* How have you changed since you were a baby? Did you look different then from the way you look now? What things can you do now that you couldn't do then?
* Do you think you will continue to change as you get older? What do you think will happen?

Encourage children to talk about how different animals change as they grow. How are these changes similar to and different from the changes butterflies go through? You might also like to paraphrase some of the butterfly information in the back of the book and point out the different species of butterflies to children.

Flower Feeders (Science)

Invite children to create butterfly feeders and see what they can attract!

1. Begin by talking with children about what butterflies eat: nectar from flowers. Point out that this nectar is sweet, like sugar. Tell children they can use real sugar to try to attract butterflies.

2. Give children each a paper plate and invite them to draw a small circle in the center, then add petals to create a daisy.

3. Next, give children each a small cup of water and help them stir in two teaspoons of sugar until it dissolves. Have them place a cotton ball in the cup to soak up the liquid.

4. Help children place the saturated cotton balls in the center of their flowers. Set the flower feeders outside in a spot where they can be observed. Check the flowers regularly to see if any butterflies have come to feed.

Note: You can also use the feeders with butterflies from a science supply house (see resources, left).

Butterfly Rhymes Word Wall (Language Arts)

Build on the rhymes in the book to create a wall of rhyming word wings.

1. First, show children how to make paper butterflies. They can fold a sheet of colored construction paper in half and draw a butterfly wing shape on one side. Then have them cut along the line they made and open the paper to make a butterfly shape.

2. Next, look through the book with children for rhyming word pairs. A few they might find are: *blow/grow, fly/sky, dip/sip,* and *eat/sweet.* Write each word pair on a butterfly, one word on each wing. Post them on an eye-level bulletin board to begin your word wall.

3. Then help children brainstorm more rhyming words to add to the wall. You might keep your focus on the butterfly theme with words such as *egg/leg, wing/spring,* and *flower/shower.*

4. Continue to add to your wall as children think of new word pairs. Use the words to create your own rhyming poem or story about butterflies.

Beautiful Butterflies (Math)

Introduce children to the concept of symmetry with these simple activities.

1. Begin by looking at the illustrations of butterflies in the book. What do children notice about the wings? Point out that the pattern on each wing is the mirror image of the pattern on the other.

2. Invite children to make their own symmetrical butterflies with coffee filters and food coloring. Have children fold a round coffee filter into quarters to make a triangle shape. Let them drop dots and lines of food coloring on the filter, then dip the triangle tip in a cup of water until the colors run. Open up the filters and lay them flat to dry. When dry, help children pinch the filter together in the middle, slide it on to a clothespin, and fan out the wings. They will see beautiful patterns!

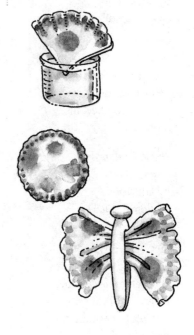

3. When children are more familiar with the concept of symmetry, challenge them to work in pairs to create symmetrical butterfly wings. Give each pair a precut paper butterfly. Have one child draw a pattern on one wing. Children can include spots, lines, and other shapes. It is then the partner's job to color the other wing to create a symmetrical pattern. You might have children hold a hand mirror in the center of the butterfly to guide them as they work.

Emerging Butterfly Puppets (Art)

With this easy craft project, children can act out how a butterfly emerges from its chrysalis.

1. Create a simple butterfly shape on card stock for a template. Help children place the template on heavy paper, trace around it, and cut it out to make a butterfly. Invite children to color in their butterflies.

2. Help children punch a small hole in the top of the butterfly and pass a short piece of pipe cleaner through it. Then help children bend the ends of the pipe cleaner up and twist together to make antennae. Have children glue their butterflies to a craft stick to make a puppet.

3. While the glue dries on the puppets, invite children to color a toilet tissue tube green or brown to look like a chrysalis. Then help children curl the wings of their butterflies inward and slide their puppets into the tubes. When they pull on the stick, the butterfly will emerge from its chrysalis and spread its wings to fly!

Follow the Caterpillar (Science and Math)

Invite children to act out the journey from egg to butterfly with the game on page 43. Copy the game board onto card stock (enlarge if possible) and invite children to color it if they wish. Provide children with small buttons (for game markers) and a penny. Invite them to play the game in small groups as follows.

1. All players place their markers on START. Take turns tossing the penny to see how many spaces to move along the caterpillar. If the penny lands heads up, move one space. If it lands tails up, move two spaces.

2. Follow any directions on the space. Use the picture as a clue and act out what it shows.

3. The first player to become a butterfly and then reach FINISH wins the game!

Follow the Caterpillar!

Start

Curl up like an egg on a leaf.

Hatch out of your egg.

Spin your chrysalis. Wrap up tight!

Eat to grow! Munch on a leaf.

Time to come out! Spread your wings.

Finish

You are a butterfly! Fly away.

Feathers for Lunch

Lois Ehlert

Feathers for Lunch

◆◆

(HARCOURT, 1990)

This whimsical rhyming story showcases a variety of colorful birds and their special calls, as a hungry cat tries to get something new to eat. But the cat makes a special sound, too—the jingle of the bell on his collar. The birds get fair warning, and all the cat catches is feathers for lunch!

Concepts and Themes

▲▲▲▲▲▲

☼ **birds**

☼ **animal sounds, bird calls**

☼ **habitats**

Before Reading

Show children the cover illustration and read the title of the book aloud. Invite children to predict what the story might be about by asking:

✳ What do you think the title means? Who might have feathers for lunch?
✳ Have you ever seen a cat chase a bird? What do you think the cat in this story will do?
✳ What might the birds do to keep from getting caught?

Next, encourage children to tell what they know about birds. Ask:

✳ What special thing can a bird do that a cat cannot?
✳ What are some of a bird's body parts? What do they use to fly? To eat?
✳ Where can you see birds in your neighborhood? What kinds of birds have you seen?
✳ What colors were they? What have you seen the birds doing?

After Reading

Encourage children to retell key parts of the story. Ask:

✳ Why did the cat catch only feathers for lunch?
✳ What did the birds do to warn each other about the cat? How did they get away?

Next, invite children to talk about the sounds birds make. Ask:

✳ Have you ever heard a bird sing or make a call? What did it sound like?
✳ Why do you think different birds make different sounds?

Page through the book again, reading the bird-call text as you point to each bird. Invite children to practice each call. You can also share the information in the back of the book about "the lunch that got away." Tell children the name of each bird, what it eats, and where it lives. Children might also be interested to know that the birds throughout the story are all illustrated at their actual size.

For the Birds (Science)

Set out treats for the birds, to see which one they like best.

1. Brainstorm with children a list of foods they think will attract birds. Ideas might include seeds, cereal, popcorn, nuts, and even fruit. Gather several clean, empty half-gallon milk cartons. Have children work in small groups to create bird feeders.

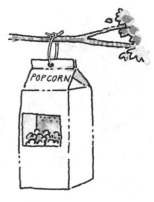

2. Help each group cut a square hole in one side of the carton and fill it with one of the foods from the list. Label each feeder with the name of the food. Which food do children think will be most popular with the birds?

3. If possible, hang the feeders from a tree near a window of your classroom, using strong string or twine. Invite children to observe any birds they attract and which feeders the birds seem to be using most. (You can also set the feeders on the ground in a safe place and go outside to check on them regularly.) At the end of a week, check the feeders to see which foods the birds took the most of. Were children's predictions correct?

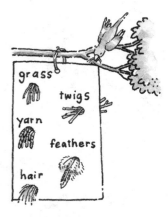

Variation: You can do a similar activity with nesting materials instead of food. Gather materials such as straw, yarn, feathers, grass, twigs, and shredded fabric. Poke small holes in a large piece of corrugated cardboard and pull the materials through so that they are hanging off the board. Set the board outside on a window ledge or hanging from a tree branch. Watch to see which materials birds like best for nests!

Bird's Nest Treats (Cooking)

Invite children to create a nest they can eat!

1. In advance, gather the foods at right. Check for peanut butter allergies. You may substitute marshmallow creme for peanut butter.

pretzel sticks	crushed graham crackers
shredded wheat cereal	melon balls
licorice whips	frozen yogurt or ice cream
peanut butter	marshmallows

2. Talk with children about any bird's nests they may have seen. What did the nests look like? What were they made of? How do children think the birds built them?

3. Set out each food on a table on a separate plate. Give children each a bowl and a spoon and invite them to use any foods they wish to create an edible version of a bird's nest. Children can press their ingredients to the sides of their bowls, using peanut butter to make them stick.

4. Encourage children to compare nests. Then add melon balls, scoops of frozen yogurt, or marshmallows to fill each nest with "eggs," and enjoy!

Growing Birdseed (Science)

Invite children to plant birdseed and see what grows.

1. Place some birdseed mixture (available at pet stores) in a sorting tray and invite children to examine it. Where do they think birdseed comes from? What might happen if they planted it? Have children sort the mixture into groups of the same type of seed.

2. Next, gather a few small (pint or half-pint) milk cartons and cut the tops off. Help children poke a hole in the bottom of each carton. Then help them fill the cartons halfway with soil and add water to moisten it. Invite children to plant the seeds, planting a different type in each container. They can label the cartons by taping a few seeds to the outside.

3. Help children loosely cover each planter with plastic wrap to keep the soil moist, and place the planters on a tray. Encourage children to check the planters daily to see if anything grows. They can keep a log and draw pictures of each plant's progress. When the plants start to sprout, you can help children poke holes in the plastic wrap to allow growth.

Go Bird-Watching (Science)

What kinds of birds live in your area? Go on a bird walk to find out.

1. Talk with children about the kinds of birds they have seen in the school neighborhood. What did the birds look like? Where have children seen them? If possible, show children a field guide of birds for your area (such as *National Audubon Society First Field Guides: Birds*, Scholastic, 1998). Look at the pictures together and have children point out those they have seen before.

2. Then go on a bird-watching walk together. If possible, go to a park or other area where you will be likely to spot a variety of birds. Encourage children to point out any birds they see on the walk, describe what they look like, and tell what they are doing. Keep a log of children's observations, noting where the bird was seen, what it looked like, and its actions.

3. Back in the classroom, look over the notes you made with children and discuss their observations. If using a field guide, look for pictures of the birds you saw and find out their names. Which birds did children see the most of? In what places did they see the most birds?

4. Invite children to draw a picture of one bird they saw on the walk, and, if possible, label it with the bird's name. Then bind the pages together to make your own field guide.

Cat and Bird Chase (Movement)

Extend the story by teaching children the names of the featured birds with this version of Red Rover. Make copies of the cat and bird necklace patterns on page 48. Cut out the pictures along the dashed lines and punch a hole in each where indicated. Give children each a picture and have them color it in if they like. Help children string yarn through the hole to make a necklace and tie it around their necks. (More than one child can have the same bird necklace, but there should be only one "cat" for the game.) Take children to an open area and teach them how to play the game as follows.

1. All children with bird necklaces form two even lines facing one another. The child with the cat necklace stands in the center and calls for a type of bird by saying, "Red rover, red rover, let *sparrows* [or other species] come over!"

2. Children with that type of bird on their necklace try to run to the other side without getting tagged by the cat! If a bird gets tagged, that player joins the cat in the center and works with him or her to try to tag the other birds. The cat continues to call out for birds, a different species each time.

3. As more birds get tagged, it will become harder and harder to get across. When all the birds have been called, children can trade necklaces and play again!

Bird Call Match-Up (Movement)

Teach children about bird calls as they sharpen their listening skills with this game.

1. Make two copies of the bird necklace patterns on page 48 and cut them out. Give each child a "secret" bird picture (making sure they will have a partner with a matching picture). Have children color their pictures. Encourage them to color the bird species with the appropriate colors, using *Feathers for Lunch* as a reference. Help children punch holes and string yarn through them to make necklaces. Have them put the necklaces on with the pictures facing in.

2. Next, help children use the book to find the sound for their bird. For instance, the blackbird's call is *o-ka-lee, o-ka-lee*; the woodpecker makes a *tap-tap-tap* sound; the goldfinch cries *su-wee, su-wee*.

3. Invite children to start at various spots in the room, then walk around as they make their bird's sound. When they find a child who is making the same sound, they can turn their necklaces over. Continue until each child has found his or her partner. Explain that real birds use their calls to find friends, too!

Cat and Bird
Necklace
Patterns

Blackbird

Cardinal

Woodpecker

Blue Jay

Oriole

Sparrow

Cat

Dove

Goldfinch

Scholastic Teaching Resources

Top Cat

◆ ◆

(HARCOURT, 1998)

Top Cat rules his people's house—until they bring home a mysterious box with a cute new cat inside. At first Top Cat does not want to share his favorite things. But he soon realizes that two cats can have even more fun—and make even more mischief—than one!

Before Reading

Invite children to share stories about any pets they may have at home. If children don't have pets, encourage them to join the discussion by talking about a pet they would like to have. Ask:

※ What kinds of pets do you have? How do you play with your pet? What special treats does your pet like?

※ If you have more than one pet, have you ever seen your pets play together? What do they do?

Then encourage children to think about their pets' feelings by asking:

※ Do you think pet animals have the same kinds of feelings people do? What are some things that might make a pet happy? What are some things that might make it sad?

Show children the cover of the book and help them read the title. What do children think it means to be the "top cat"? Invite them to share any predictions they have about the story.

After Reading

Encourage children to talk about Top Cat's feelings, and help them relate the story to their own experiences. Ask:

※ Why do you think Top Cat was upset when a new cat came to his house?

※ Have you ever welcomed someone new to your family or to your home? How did you feel about it? What did you do?

※ Is it sometimes hard to share your favorite things with sisters, brothers, or friends? Why?

Then invite children to talk about the ways Top Cat solved his problem. Ask:

※ How did Top Cat learn to be friends with the new cat? What kinds of things did they do together?

※ What kinds of activities do you like to do by yourself? What kinds of things are more fun when you do them with a friend?

Concepts and Themes

▲▲▲▲▲▲

☼ pets, cats

☼ animal behavior

☼ sharing and acceptance

☼ welcoming someone new

Welcome Wreath (Social Studies)

Top Cat had trouble giving the new cat a warm welcome, until he learned how much fun it could be to play with a new friend. Children can create a wreath to show that all are welcome to join the fun in their classroom.

1. Talk with children about how it feels to be in a new environment—to come to a new school, meet new classmates, or move to a new town. What are some ways to make a newcomer feel welcome? Sharing and playing together are always a good start!

2. Make one copy of the heart pattern on page 53 for each child. Invite children to write their name and draw a picture of themselves doing something to welcome a friend or visitor, such as waving hello or sharing a toy. (If you have access to a camera, you might like to take photographs of children showing how they welcome friends, and have them paste their picture on the heart.)

3. Cut a large circle of tagboard and cut a hole in the middle to create a wreath. Have children paste their hearts around the circle. Hang your wreath on the classroom door to let both old friends and new ones know they are welcome!

Feline Feelings Charades (Dramatic Play)

As children learned in the story, cats have feelings, too! Invite children to act out animal feelings in a game of charades.

1. Talk with children about the feelings that Top Cat and the new cat had in the story. What words would children use to describe these feelings? For instance, did Top Cat start out angry? Was the new cat scared at first? How did they feel by the end of the story?

2. Write several emotion words on index cards, such as *happy, sad, scared, angry,* and *surprised.* You might also draw a simple face on each card to show the emotion.

3. Place the cards in a paper bag. Invite children to take turns coming up to pick a card, and have them act out the emotion for the group. Children can pretend to be a cat as they act out a scenario—for instance, a cat might be happy playing with a ball of yarn or scared when she sees a dog! Encourage children to use body language to act out their scenarios: They can meow, but no talking allowed! Invite the rest of the group to guess the emotion and what is happening in each scenario.

4. When each card has been picked, you might choose a different animal for children to play-act (such as a dog or a bird) and play a new round.

People and Pets (Math and Social Studies)

What do people have in common with animals? Create a diagram to find out.

1. Create a Venn diagram on chart paper or tagboard. Write the phrase "People need…" above one circle, the phrase "Pets need…" above the other circle, and the phrase "Both need…" above the intersection.

2. Talk with children about things they need, such as food, water, and shelter. What kinds of things do pets need? As children suggest different needs, ask them whether it should be written in the People, Pets, or Both section and have them explain why they think so.

3. When your diagram is full, discuss it with children: How are people and pets similar? How are they different? You might also create a second diagram, substituting the word *like* for the word *need*.

Who's the Top Cat? (Social Studies)

Everyone needs to feel special. Give each child in your class a chance to be Top Cat!

1. Talk with children about how Top Cat felt in the beginning of the story: Sometimes it can be hard to share the spotlight. But everyone can have a chance to feel special—all they have to do is take turns!

2. Choose an eye-level bulletin board on which to spotlight a new "Top Cat" each week. You can post a picture of the child and samples of his or her artwork or writing. Invite the rest of the class to celebrate the Top Cat as well—they can draw pictures and write or dictate messages telling what makes this child special and why he or she is a good friend. Post children's pictures and messages on the board and share them throughout the week.

3. At the end of the week, let the Top Cat thank his or her friends and share what the experience felt like. Then it's time to hand the spotlight over to a new Top Cat! Continue to rotate until each child has had a chance to shine.

Additional Resources

Charlie Anderson
by Barbara Abercrombie
(Margaret K. McElderry, 1990)

When two girls adopt a cat who appears at their door every evening, they wonder where he goes during the day. When they discover that the cat also lives with another family who lets him out at night, they realize that cats—and people—can call more than one place "home."

Hondo & Fabian
by Peter McCarty
(Henry Holt, 2002)

What do pet cats and dogs do all day? Hondo the dog and Fabian the cat may have fun in different ways, but at the end of the day they are part of the same family.

My Cats Nick & Nora
by Isabelle Harper
(Scholastic, 1995)

Children will delight in experiencing an ordinary but hilarious day in the life of two pet cats and the children who love them.

No No, Jo!
by Kate McMullan
(HarperCollins, 1998)

Jo the cat tries hard to be "the world's most helpful kitten," but her well-intentioned efforts always seem to cause trouble for her family of humans. Children will enjoy repeating the refrain and lifting the flap on each page to see Jo's mischief.

Our Pets Graph (Math)

What kinds of pets do children have at home? Create a class graph to see which are the most common.

1. As in the Before Reading section, survey children to see what kinds of pets they have. Write the names of the animals as column-headings on a sheet of chart paper or tagboard. Be sure to include a column for "No Pets."

2. Let children take turns coming up to the chart to mark any pets they have. They can make a check mark under each appropriate column.

3. When the graph is complete, discuss the results. Which pet is the most common? Which is the least common? Invite children to talk about what their different pets need and how they help take care of them. How is each pet alike and different?

4. For a fun extension, you might also create a "dream pets" graph. What fantasy pet would most children like to have? Which is more popular, a dinosaur or a rhino?

Cat Coupons (Social Studies)

Top Cat learned an important lesson in the story: that sharing can be fun! Invite children to create "sharing coupons" for their classmates.

1. Make copies of the coupon on page 53, one for each child. Read the rhyme with children and ask them what they might do to show their friends that they like to share and play with them. For instance, they might share a toy, read a book together, or play a game.

2. Assign each child a "secret friend" to create a coupon for. You might choose to do this randomly, or pair off children who don't often spend time together. Help children write or dictate a phrase to complete the sentence, such as "share my snack" or "do a puzzle." Then have them fill in their name and their friend's name.

3. When children have gone home for the day, slip each coupon in the recipient's cubby. When children arrive the next day, they will have a nice surprise! Encourage children to "make good" on their coupons to each other throughout the day.

4. You might also choose to keep a supply of coupons in your writing center to inspire acts of kindness at any time. Children can give each other coupons as presents or thank-you notes.

To: Jessie
I will play a game
with
From: Fiona

Friends old and new, we welcome you!

Welcome
Wreath

Name:

_____

Cat Coupon

To: _____

I like to share and play with you! Here is something I will do.

I will _____

_____ with you!

From: _____

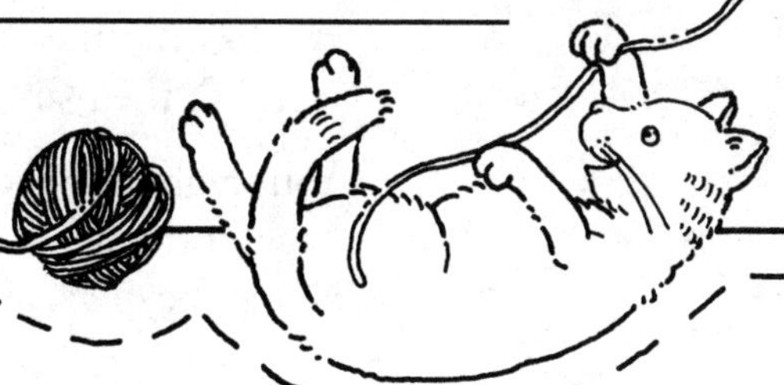

Nuts to You!

(HARCOURT, 1993)

When an industrious squirrel climbs up the brick wall of a building and into an apartment window, digging up flower boxes as he goes, we see that nature is a part of city life as well as country life. But a squirrel does not belong in an apartment—and the child who lives there hatches a "nutty" plan to get him back outside where he belongs!

Concepts and Themes

▲▲▲▲▲▲

☼ squirrels
☼ nuts
☼ habitats
☼ problem-solving

Before Reading

Begin by talking with children about the kinds of animals they see in their home neighborhoods. Whether they live in a town, city, or rural area, animals are all around them if they know where to look! Ask:

※ What kinds of living things can you see near your home? Have you ever seen insects or birds in your yard, on your street, or in a nearby park?

※ Have you ever seen any other animals (besides pets) in your neighborhood? What kind? Where did you see them?

Next, show children the cover of the book. Do they recognize the animal in the illustration? Ask:

※ Have you ever seen squirrels near where you live? What were they doing?

※ What would you do if a squirrel got into your house or apartment? How might you get the squirrel to go back outside?

After Reading

First, encourage children to talk about the setting of the story. Point out that the story took place in a city neighborhood. Ask:

※ What kinds of nature can you see in the city? Were you surprised to see flowers and trees in this story? Why or why not?

※ What animals besides squirrels might you see in a city neighborhood?

Next, invite children to retell the sequence of the story. Ask:

※ How did the squirrel get inside the apartment? Why did the people who lived there want to get him out?

※ How did the child get the squirrel to go back outside? Why do you think the plan worked?

You might also like to share with children some of the "squirrel talk" in the back of the book, which contains information about squirrels' body parts, where they live, and what they eat.

A Tree for the Squirrels (Science)

Want to see squirrels in action? Decorate a tree with squirrel treats to attract these nimble creatures. If possible, choose a tree outside your classroom window. Alternatively, you can decorate any nearby tree and visit it regularly to observe the squirrels. There are several kinds of tree treats you can create:

◎ Create cereal garlands to hang from the branches. Children can string cereal loops through a length of yarn, then tie the ends together and hang the garlands. You may see squirrels picking pieces of cereal off the string, or doing a few acrobatic moves to remove the whole garland!

◎ Corn also attracts squirrels. In advance, hammer a nail through a dried corncob, then remove the nail to create a hole. (You can also use a drill.) Help children thread a length of thick, strong twine through the hole and hang it from your tree. Most squirrels will go to great lengths to get to the corn—even if they have to hang upside down!

◎ Encourage children to observe the squirrels, noting how they move and what body parts they use to get the treats. Do the squirrels eat their treats right away or hide them in a safe place for storage? Children might keep science journals of their squirrel observations. Encourage them to draw pictures of the squirrels they saw and illustrate what they were doing.

Variation: If you do not have access to a tree, you can attract squirrels simply by scattering nuts on the ground. Some nuts you might try are acorns, hickory nuts, walnuts, and pecans. Tell children to observe the squirrels from a safe distance; they must never try to feed a squirrel by hand. You might also try leaving a row of nuts on a windowsill or ledge outside your room and see who stops by for a snack. Just be sure to keep the window closed, or you may get a classroom visit from an uninvited guest!

Nuts About Nuts (Math)

Reinforce sorting and matching skills with a nutty activity! Before doing this activity, make sure no children have nut allergies. Collect a wide variety of unshelled nuts, such as acorns, walnuts, pecans, brazil nuts, and pistachios. Provide children with sorting trays and invite them to sort the nuts by a variety of criteria, such as shape, size, and color. Then crack the nuts open (keeping the shells as intact as possible) and separate the meats from the shells. Mix them up and challenge children to guess which nut came from each shell!

Find That Nut! (Movement)

Squirrels hide their nuts to prepare for lean, cold winters; then they find their hidden stash and feed on it throughout the season. Invite children to role-play squirrels in a nut-hunting game.

1. Gather several unshelled nuts, such as acorns, walnuts, pecans, and beechnuts. (Alternatively, you can make paper nuts from different shades of brown construction paper.)

2. Divide the class into pairs, and give each pair a different nut. Assign one child to be the "nut hider" and the other to be the "squirrel." As all the squirrels close their eyes, the hiders place their nuts in secret locations around the classroom. When all the nuts have been hidden, the hiders call out "Nuts to You!" and it's time for the squirrels to get to work!

3. Encourage children to move like squirrels as they hunt for their nuts. As the squirrels hunt, the hiders can guide them through the room giving clues—for instance, "Hop closer to the bookcase" or "Jump to the door."

4. As squirrels find their nuts, they call out "Nuts to Me!" Then it's time for the partners to switch roles and play again.

There's an Animal in My House! (Language Arts)

Children will be interested to know that *Nuts to You* was inspired by a real experience the author had with one of the squirrels in her neighborhood. Have children ever had the experience of finding an "uninvited guest" in their home? Invite them to create their own stories about surprise animal visitors.

1. Write the following incomplete sentences on a sheet of paper and make a copy for each child:

   There's a _____ in my house and it's running all about.

   I'm going to _____ to get him out!

2. Invite children to write or dictate words to fill in the first blank. What kinds of animals might sneak into their homes? In addition to squirrels, ideas might include a bird, a bug, or a mouse. Children might also enjoy writing about an unlikely animal visitor, such as a giraffe or a hippo!

3. Next, help children complete the second sentence. The child in *Nuts to You* came up with a special plan to get her squirrel visitor back outside. What might children do to lure their animals out of the house? Would they leave a trail of food? Tie a leash around its neck and walk it out the door? Encourage children to be creative with their ideas—their plans might be realistic or just plain silly!

4. Invite children to draw illustrations to go with their stories. Display pages on a bulletin board or bind them together to make a class book.

City Nature (Social Studies)

Nuts to You is an unusual Lois Ehlert book in that it takes place in a city environment. However, she still includes her trademark love of nature: The pages are alive with living and growing things. Help children celebrate nature with a mural!

1. Invite children to look through the book for signs of nature in the city, such as trees, flowers in window boxes, birds, and, of course, squirrels! Then invite children to create a mural showing how nature can thrive in the city. Provide a large sheet of craft paper, and encourage them to draw or paint a city scene: They might include tall buildings, sidewalks, cars on busy streets, and so on.

2. Then invite them to add natural elements to the mural. For instance, they might draw trees lining the sidewalks, grass sprouting from cracks in the pavement, garden boxes in building windows, and animals such as pigeons and squirrels. Display the completed mural on a wall of the classroom and invite children to discuss their work. Do children think trees, flowers, and animals are an important part of a neighborhood? How can these natural things make a city a nicer place to live?

Nutty Squirrel Treats (Cooking)

These snacks are sure to please the little squirrels in your classroom! Invite children to help read the recipe and take turns following each step. Be sure to check for nut allergies before serving. You will need:

Nutty Squirrel Treats

1 1/2 cups graham cracker crumbs
1 cup powdered sugar
1/4 cup melted butter

1 cup chopped nuts (any kind)
1/4 cup undiluted frozen juice (any kind)

1. In a large bowl, combine the cracker crumbs, powdered sugar, butter, and nuts.
2. Add the juice and mix thoroughly.
3. Form spoonfuls of the mixture into small balls.
4. Roll the balls on a cookie sheet that has been sprinkled with additional powdered sugar.

Acorn Painting (Art)

You can make paint from acorns! Crack open about a dozen acorns. Let children examine the insides. Help them collect the yellow meal from the inside of the acorns and mix it with 1/2 teaspoon of cooking oil to create a paint paste.

Additional Resources

Merle the High Flying Squirrel
by Bill Peet
(Houghton Mifflin, 1983)

Follow Merle the squirrel as he travels west from the city to the forests.

Squirrel Is Hungry
by Satoshi Kitamura
(Farrar Straus & Giroux, 1996)

Squirrel is on a mission to find a place to store his walnut: Should he hide it in a bird's nest, under a rock, or in the hollow of a tree? Children will enjoy following Squirrel on his journey to find the perfect spot.

Squirrels
by Brian Wildsmith
(Franklin Watts, 1997)

Did you know that squirrels use their tails as parachutes when jumping down from a tree? Children will delight in this book filled with fascinating facts.

A Squirrel's Tale
by Richard Fowler
(Educational Development Corporation, 1984)

Children will love helping a squirrel find his hidden nuts in this innovative, interactive book. By pushing the squirrel through a slot on each page, they help in his search.

Color Zoo
(HARPERCOLLINS, 1989)

❖❖

Color Farm
(HARPERCOLLINS, 1990)

Concepts and Themes

▲▲▲▲▲▲▲

✿ **zoo animals**

✿ **farm animals**

✿ **colors**

✿ **shapes**

Color Zoo, a Caldecott Honor book, introduces shapes, colors, and zoo animals in a dazzling feat of graphic design. Each animal is represented by colorful geometric shapes, which are cut out of the pages. When the page is turned and the shape is removed, a new animal is revealed—along with the name of the previous shape. The author's follow-up *Color Farm* follows the same format, this time with farm animals. Each book has simple text labels, allowing the concepts to take center stage.

Before Reading

Tap children's prior knowledge of zoo and farm animals by asking:

✳ Have you ever been to the zoo? What kinds of animals did you see there? Which did you like best?

✳ Have you ever seen a farm? What kinds of animals live on a farm? Are they different from the animals you can see in the zoo?

✳ If you could spend the day either at the zoo or on a farm, which would you choose? Why?

Next, show children the covers of the books. As you examine each cover with the class, ask:

✳ What animal do you see? What shapes is the animal made of? What colors?

✳ What other animals do you think you might see in the "color zoo"? How about on the "color farm"?

After Reading

Talk with children about the unique design of the books. Ask:

✳ Were you surprised to see that animal faces could be made out of shapes? If you were to make your own animal out of shapes, which shape would you use for each part?

✳ How did these animals look different from the way real animals look? For instance, what colors can you see on a real tiger? What colors did you see on the tiger in *Color Zoo*?

Page through the books once more, this time without reading the text labels. Invite children to name each animal and point out the colors and shapes they see. Which animals, colors, and shapes are children's favorites?

Extension Activities

That's a Horse of a Different Color! (Art)

The animals in *Color Zoo* and *Color Farm* are made up of bright, imaginative colors. What would the world look like if it were filled with pink elephants, green cats, and purple cows? Find out with this activity.

1. Gather an empty shoe box, several sheets of brightly colored cellophane (red, orange, yellow, blue, green, purple), and a variety of small toy animals. Cut a small viewing hole at one end of the shoebox. At the other end, cut out a large rectangle from the lid and tape a sheet of cellophane over the space.

2. Invite children to sit in a bright area of the room, place a toy animal inside the box and close the lid. When they look through the viewing hole, they will see the animal in a different color! Encourage children to look at several different animals and describe what they see. Then change the color of cellophane on the box lid and try it again.

3. When children have viewed a variety of animals and colors, invite them to draw or paint pictures of their favorite combinations (for instance, a blue horse or a purple pig). Display children's work on a bulletin board for a wildly colored menagerie!

Animal Shape Collages (Art and Math)

Children can approximate the technique in the book by creating their own animals out of colored shapes.

1. In advance, cut a wide variety of shapes from colored construction paper, including triangles, squares, circles, ovals, and hexagons. Create several colors and sizes of each shape.

2. Provide children with sheets of plain white construction paper, glue, and a supply of paper shapes, and invite them to create an animal. Children can look in the books for initial ideas, but encourage them to be creative and try their own combinations. They might like to experiment with moving different shapes around the paper before gluing them down.

3. When children have finished, invite them to count how many of each shape they used to make their animal. Then have them turn their paper over and write or dictate the name of the animal and the number of each shape they used.

4. Children can then trade collages with a partner. Invite them to guess the animal and count the number of each shape, then turn the paper over to check their guesses.

Shape and Color Scavenger Hunt (Math and Science)

Animal faces aren't the only places to find shapes and colors. Help children practice shape and color recognition by going on scavenger hunts.

◎ For a shape scavenger hunt, prepare a record sheet by drawing several shapes down the left side of a sheet of paper (such as a circle, oval, triangle, square, and rectangle). Make one copy of the sheet for each child. Then invite children to look around the classroom for each shape. Encourage children to think creatively—shapes are everywhere! The door might be a rectangle, a windowpane might be a square, and another child's face might be an oval! Have children make a tick next to each shape on the sheet as they find examples. Then gather as a group and discuss children's findings: What shapes were most commonly found? Which were least common? In what unusual places did children find shapes?

◎ For a color scavenger hunt, prepare record sheets by drawing a number of "paint blot" outlines down the left side of a sheet of paper. Make one copy for each child, and have children color each blot with a different-colored marker, such as red, orange, yellow, green, blue, and purple. Then have them go on a scavenger hunt following the procedure above.

Farm and Zoo Animal Sort (Math)

Animals are a great venue for sorting activities. Collect a variety of animal pictures (nature magazines are a good resource) and cut them out. You can also have children draw their own pictures of animals. Invite children to sort the pictures in a variety of ways, such as the ones listed below.

◎ Create a Venn diagram on the floor with two intersecting circles of yarn. Designate one circle for farm animals, one for zoo animals, and the intersection for animals that might be found in either place. Place the pile of pictures next to the diagram and invite children to take turns choosing an animal and placing it in the diagram. Encourage children to explain their choices: Why would a sheep be more likely to be found on a farm? Why would a tiger belong in the zoo section?

◎ Place several yarn circles in separate spots on the floor. Invite children to create their own criteria for each circle and sort the animals accordingly. For instance, children might use two circles to sort animals by number of legs (two or four), or they might use three circles to sort animals by texture (fur, feathers, or smooth skin). They might also use several circles to sort animals by color.

Animal Shape Snacks (Art and Cooking)

Invite children to build an animal's face out of shapes they can eat! In advance, gather the following:

circular cookie cutter

bread

cheese slices, cut into triangles

peanut butter (or marshmallow creme)

raisins

thin pretzel sticks

shredded carrots

1. Give each child a paper plate and a slice of bread. Let children take turns using the cookie cutter to make a bread circle, and have them place it on the plate.

2. Next, invite children to spread peanut butter on the circle. Let each child take three raisins and place them on the peanut butter to make eyes and a nose. Then let children add pretzel sticks for whiskers and sprinkle shredded carrots for fur, if they wish. Finally, have children place two cheese triangle slices on top of their animal face for ears.

3. Before children eat their snacks, invite them to tell about their animal. The face might belong to a kitten, a dog, or even a lion. Also encourage children to talk about the shapes they used: cheese triangles, a bread circle, and oval raisins. Have them point to each shape, name it, then eat and enjoy!

Animal Cracker Charades (Dramatic Play)

Use a box of animal crackers for a quick and easy snack time charades game. Let a child pick a cracker out of the box and eat it (without showing the group the animal). Invite children to "become" the animal they ate, acting out its movements and the sounds it makes. The first child to guess the animal correctly gets to pick the next cracker!

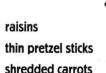

Market Day

(HARCOURT, 2000)

In rhyming verse, this book tells a simple story of a family that travels from their farm to the town square market and back again. At the farmers market, they buy and sell fruits and vegetables. At the end of the day, it's time to eat their goods! The unique illustrations are photographed collages made up of various pieces of folk art from the author's personal collection.

Concepts and Themes

- ☼ markets
- ☼ farms
- ☼ buying and selling
- ☼ folk art

Before Reading

Begin by showing children the cover of the book and reading the title aloud. Do children know what a market is? Tap children's prior knowledge of markets by asking:

* Where does your family go to buy the food you eat? Do you go to a supermarket?
* Where do you think the food at the supermarket comes from?
* Where are the fruits and vegetables grown? Who grows them?

Explain to children that fruits and vegetables are grown on farms. The farmers grow the food and then sell it to a store (such as a supermarket) or to other people. Find out if any children have ever been to a farmers market. Explain that it is a place where farmers gather to sell the food they grow. Ask:

* What kinds of foods do you think you might see at a farmers market?

After Reading

Talk with children about the trip described in the story. Ask:

* Do you think it would be fun to visit a farmers market? How might it be different from going to a supermarket?
* If you could meet the farmers who grow your food, what would you say to them? What questions might you ask?

Next, discuss the book's illustrations with children. Page through the book again, inviting children to point to their favorite pieces of artwork. As children point out different objects, ask:

* What do you think this was made from? If you wanted to make a piece of art like this, what materials would you use? How would you do it?

You might like to turn to the back of the book and read the information about the objects children are most interested in, telling them the materials that were used and where the objects came from.

Class Marketplace (Social Studies and Math)

Introduce children to the concepts of buying and selling by setting up your own "farmers market" in the classroom.

1. Talk with children about things that are sold at a farmers market. In addition to fruits and vegetables, farmers also often sell flowers and plants from their gardens, and foods made by the animals they keep, such as milk from the cows, honey from the bees, and eggs from the chickens.

2. Divide the class into small groups and help each group of "farmers" to brainstorm items they will sell. Then help children gather or create their goods. Children might use play food and recyclable items such as clean, empty food containers. They can also create produce out of Play-Doh, or simply draw pictures of the items they'd like to sell and cut them out. Help each group set up a "stand" at the market in different areas of the classroom. They can set out their goods on a table and create price tags with sticky notes. You can even include a scale for weighing food.

3. Invite one group of farmers to leave their stand and become customers. Provide them with play money and let them visit each stand to "buy" different items. Encourage customers to ask the farmers about the goods they are selling. Groups take turns until each group has had a chance both to buy and to sell.

Making Folk Art (Art)

Market Day is illustrated with folk art—handmade objects that people create from the materials they find around them. Invite children to use items they find in the classroom to create their own versions of folk art.

1. Look through the book with children and invite them to name the different materials used to create various objects. Then encourage children to brainstorm items in the classroom that they might use to create their own folk art. In addition to paper, paints, and fabric, children might use empty milk cartons or lunch trays, bottle caps, broken crayons, bits of yarn and string, and so on.

2. Gather the materials and invite children to examine them. How can they use them to create a piece of art? They might create an abstract piece, such as a collage of bottle caps glued to a plastic foam lunch tray and sprinkled with decorative glitter. Or they might create a specific item, such as a sock puppet with button eyes and fabric scrap hair. Display children's work in a classroom "folk art museum."

Additional Resources

Catch That Goat!
by Polly Alakija
(Barefoot Books, 2002)

In this unique counting book, a little girl's mischievous goat escapes in a Nigerian street market—and one item mysteriously disappears from each vendor's stand.

Market!
by Ted Lewin
(Lothrop Lee & Shepard, 1996)

From Nepal to New York City, take a trip around the globe to see what people buy and sell at the market.

Market Day
by Eve Bunting
(HarperCollins, 1996)

Children will enjoy following a little girl and her friend through the special market that takes place once each month in their Irish village.

To Market, to Market
by Anne Miranda
(Harcourt, 1997)

In this hilarious version of the traditional rhyme, an ambitious shopper goes to the market to buy not only a "fat pig" but a duck, a goat, and a cow as well!

A Lois Ehlert Celebration: Culminating Activities

The following activities are ideas for wrapping up your author study. You can use any or all of these activities to celebrate the books of Lois Ehlert and all that children have learned from reading them!

Put on a Show

Dramatizing a story is a great way to reinforce children's understanding of its sequence and concepts. Divide the class into small groups and invite each group to act out a different book. Some stories, such as *Top Cat* or *Feathers for Lunch*, will lend themselves well to the creation of dialogue: Children can take on roles of different animal characters and invent their own "script." Other stories, such as *Planting a Rainbow* or *Waiting for Wings*, might best be acted out through movement. For instance, children might pretend to be seeds, curling up on the floor and then "sprouting" upward until they become beautiful flowers; or they might act out the journey from egg to butterfly, crawling as caterpillars, spinning a chrysalis, then spreading their wings to fly. Children can gather or create simple props and costumes for their shows.

Class Favorites

Invite children to create a graph of their favorite Lois Ehlert books. Write the titles the class has read down the left side of a large sheet of tagboard. Read each title aloud to children and help them recall the story and illustrations. Provide children with large, unlined index cards, and have them illustrate a scene from the book they enjoyed most. Then invite children to come up to the graph and attach their card next to the appropriate title. When the graph is complete, discuss the results. Which book was the most popular? Also invite children to tell why they chose the book they selected as their favorite.

Natural Snacks

Celebrate Lois Ehlert's love of nature by serving all-natural foods at the party. In addition to mixed nuts (*Nuts to You!*), fruits and vegetables (*Eating the Alphabet*) and, of course, vegetable soup (*Growing Vegetable Soup*), children might enjoy creating other natural snacks, such as trail mix made with sunflower seeds and raisins or a salad made with leafy lettuce and ripe, fruity tomatoes. You might also introduce children to all-natural versions of old favorites, such as natural rather than processed peanut butter and whole-fruit preserves instead of jelly. How do these versions differ from the products children may be more familiar with? Encourage children to describe tastes, textures, and colors as they enjoy their feast of nature's bounty!